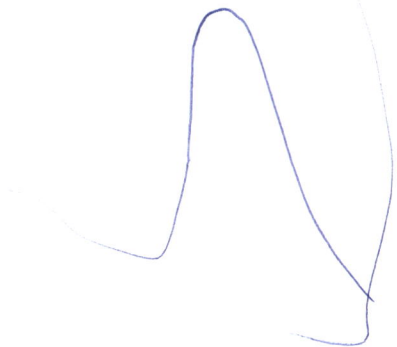

ECO-PLANES

by Ellis M. Reed

Consultant: Beth Gambro
Reading Specialist, Yorkville, Illinois

BEARPORT
PUBLISHING

Minneapolis, Minnesota

Teaching Tips

Before Reading

- Look at the cover of the book. Discuss the picture and the title.

- Ask readers to brainstorm a list of what they already know about planes. What can they expect to see in this book?

- Go on a picture walk, looking through the pictures to discuss vocabulary and make predictions about the text.

During Reading

- Read for purpose. Encourage readers to think about what makes a plane an eco-plane as they are reading.

- Ask readers to look for the details of the book. What are they learning about things that can make planes better for Earth?

- If readers encounter an unknown word, ask them to look at the sounds in the word. Then, ask them to look at the rest of the page. Are there any clues to help them understand?

After Reading

- Encourage readers to pick a buddy and reread the book together.

- Ask readers to name something that can make planes eco-friendly. Find the page that tells about this thing.

- Ask readers to write or draw something they learned about eco-planes.

Credits: Cover and title page, © The Asahi Shimbun/Getty Images and © CGiHeart/iStock; 3, © CGi Heart/Shutterstock; 5, © Skycolors/Shutterstock; 7, © VanderWolf Images/Shutterstock; 8–9, © VDWI Aviation/Alamy and © jannoon028/Shutterstock; 10–11, © Scharfsinn/Shutterstock and © aPhoenix photographer/Shutterstock; 13, © Thierry GRUN - Aero/Alamy; 14–15, © Steve Mann/Shutterstock; 16–17, © Moisieiev Igor/Shutterstock and © aPhoenix photographer/Shutterstock; 18–19, © ugurhan/Getty Images; 21, © ullstein bild Dtl./Getty Images and © Mike_Pellinni/iStock; 22, © Vadim Pacajev/Alamy and © elenavolkova/iStock; 23TL, © Thierry GRUN - Aero/Alamy; 23TM, © Ollie Desforges/iStock; 23TR, © Valerii Zadorozhnyi/Shutterstock; 23BL, © lsannes/iStock; 23BM, © Jana Richter/iStock; and 23BR, © Jag_cz/iStock.

Library of Congress Cataloging-in-Publication Data is available at www.loc.gov or upon request from the publisher.

ISBN: 978-1-63691-746-7 (hardcover)
ISBN: 978-1-63691-753-5 (paperback)
ISBN: 978-1-63691-760-3 (ebook)

For more information, write to Bearport Publishing, 5357 Penn Avenue South, Minneapolis, MN 55419. Printed in the United States of America.

Contents

Flying High

Look up in the sky!

A special plane zooms past.

Whoosh!

It is an eco-plane!

Many planes use **fuel** to fly high in the sky.

This puts bad **gases** into the air.

But eco-planes are different.

New eco-planes may use less fuel than old planes.

How do they do it?

The planes are less heavy.

They do not have to work as hard to go.

Some eco-planes use fuels that are made from plants.

They put fewer bad gases into the air.

This is better for Earth.

There are even eco-planes that use no fuel.

They fly with **electricity** from a **battery**.

The battery gives the planes **power**.

Say electricity like
i-lek-TRIS-i-tee

Electric planes are also quieter.

They make less noise **pollution**.

Loud noises can hurt Earth in many ways.

Say pollution like
puh-LOO-shuhn

Noise pollution can make people sick.

It can also scare animals away from their food.

Quieter eco-planes do not do this.

Eco-planes are used
for many reasons.

Some carry people.

Others bring food and
mail all over the world.

But they are all
helping Earth.

Next time you look to the sky, pay attention.

You might see an eco-plane.

Let's all go green with eco-planes!

SAFRAN

SIEMENS

F-WATT

Green Planes

Wing

Body

Tail

Battery

Glossary

battery something put in a machine to give it electricity

electricity a form of energy that can make things work

fuel a liquid used to make some planes go

gases things that float in the air

pollution things that cause harm to animals and people

power the ability to do something

Index

Read More

Duling, Kaitlyn. *Airplanes (How It Works).* Minneapolis: Bellwether Media, 2022.

Sabelko, Rebecca. *Flight Attendants (Community Helpers).* Minneapolis: Bellwether Media, 2020.

Learn More Online

1. Go to **www.factsurfer.com** or scan the QR code below.
2. Enter "**Eco-Planes**" into the search box.
3. Click on the cover of this book to see a list of websites.

About the Author

Ellis M. Reed loves learning about new ways to go green. She lives in Minnesota with her cat. She flies on a plane to visit family in Florida.